THE COMPLETE B

FACE PAIN

THE COMPLETE BOOK OF
FACE PAINTING

Step-by-step projects for fantastic fun faces

by

EBURY PRESS

LONDON

First published in 1996

1 3 5 7 9 10 8 6 4 2

This edition published in 1996 by Ebury Press, Random House,
20 Vauxhall Bridge Road, London SW1V 2SA

Random House Australia (Pty) Limited,
20 Alfred Street, Milsons Point,
Sydney, New South Wales 2061, Australia

Random House New Zealand Limited,
18 Poland Road, Glenfield,
Auckland 10, New Zealand

Random House South Africa (Pty) Limited,
PO Box 337, Bergvlei,
South Africa

Random House UK Limited Reg. No. 954009

A CIP catalogue record for this book is available from the
British Library.

ISBN 009 181408 1

Edited by Nicky Hodge
Designed by Jerry Goldie Graphic Design
Photographed by Karl Adamson

Colour separations by Globalcolour, London
Printed and bound in Portugal by Printer Portugesa, Lisbon

**Sherrill Leathem of MIMICKS runs professional training
courses and children's workshops in face painting.
For information, contact MIMICKS,
PO Box 116, Eastleigh, Hampshire SO53 4ZN.**

CONTENTS

ＩNTRODUCTION

Turn a boy into a lion and he will find it hard not to let out a mighty roar. With the face of a queen to hide behind, even the most shy girl will take on a new personality. Give an adult a mask and they too can relive their childhood, becoming their favourite film star, or the clown they once saw at the circus.

By entering the creative world of face painting you can cast aside reality and make beasts out of beauties, transform schoolkids into superheroes and age the young before they get old.

All ages like to roleplay and fantasize and, with the help of MIMICKS FACE PAINTING, you can create a cast of new characters to fulfil your wildest dreams.

GETTING STARTED

Take a good look at your own face in the mirror and discover how it works. Feel the bone structure and the contrasting fleshy areas. Even without face paint you can imagine the scowl of a dreadful monster or the coy smile of a demure princess. Try grinning like a crazy clown or growling like a tiger and then see what happens to your eyes, eyebrows, mouth and chin. You can then use face paints to emphasize your features in lots of wonderful ways to create hundreds of different expressions.

Face painting has never been so much fun. With this book to guide you, a set of face paints and a few brushes, you will soon have all the techniques and ideas you need to create fantastic faces.

IMPORTANT

Check before starting that the person to be painted does not have a skin allergy, eye infection or cold sore. Face paints should never be used under such circumstances.

PRODUCTS

The best face paints to use are water-based as these are easy to apply and give a professional result. By mixing the basic colours together in a lid or on a plate, you can make new shades. Once dry, these paints give a matt appearance and hardly rub off unless they get wet. To remove water-based paints, simply wash off with soap and water. Use a mild cleansing cream to remove paint around and under the eyes.

Good quality brushes should be used, such as sable brushes, as they are easy to control and maintain their flexibility. You will need an assortment of brushes to paint different strokes. Flat-edged bristles can be used for blending and creating large areas of colour, whilst rounded and pointed bristles are used for making fine lines and adding intricate details.

Synthetic or natural sponges are used to apply a base layer of colour. Fine or coarse stipple sponges are good for creating special effects such as bruising, stubble, or for softening areas of paint.

To add instant sparkle to your work apply a quick drying glitter gel — available in a variety of colours.

The products below can be purchased from most good toy, art and theatrical shops. You will find a list of suppliers at the back of the book.

Check that you have the following basic items before you start:

Table and chair

Water-based face paints

Old towel or cloth — to place your paints on

Sponges — one for each different colour

Brushes — assorted shapes and sizes

Water in a bowl or dish — plus access to a fresh supply of water

Lid or plate — for mixing colours

Baby wipes — to clean dirty faces

Overall or towel — to protect clothing

Grey make-up pencil — for outlining

Mirror — perhaps most important of all

For more adventurous designs you will also need:

Glitter gel — to add sparkle

Stipple sponges — fine and coarse

Coloured make-up powders

Powder brushes

The Basic Technique

All your equipment, including the paints, should be placed within easy reach of the hand you are using to paint. Protect clothing by placing an overall or towel around the child's shoulders and, if necessary, tie the hair back with a hair band.

Begin by cleansing the face with a baby wipe. Next apply a base layer of paint using a damp sponge (see opposite). You can add further colours to the base to create different tones over the face, either by creating blocks of colour or by blending colours for a softer effect. Use one sponge per colour and, after use, wash them thoroughly in a bowl of mild soapy water.

When the base is dry, it is often helpful to outline your design first with a soft grey make-up pencil. To fill in the details of your design you should hold your brush like a pencil, resting your little finger comfortably somewhere on the face as this will provide balance to your hand. Paint in the lightest colours first and where possible start at the forehead and work down.

Face painting is made easier by sitting the child on a sturdy table as shown here. This is the best position, as it is possible to move round to paint each side of the face without twisting the child's head to and fro.

Take great care when outlining the delicate eye area, especially if children are finding it hard to sit still.

With a little practice you will soon be able to apply an even base in no time at all, leaving you free to experiment. As your painting skills progress, try creating your own designs.

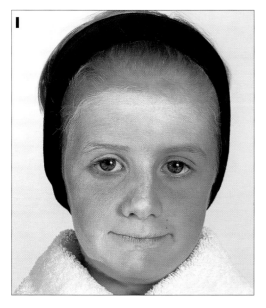

1 Take a damp, but not wet, sponge and stroke it over the paint a couple of times to build up a layer. Test its consistency on the back of your hand as it should not be too wet or the paint will streak. Start at the forehead and work downward in quick sweeping movements. Pay attention to the creases around the eyes, nose and mouth.

2 Once satisfied with your base, you may wish to add a second border tone. Blend the edges together with soft dabbing strokes. If the base starts to streak or bubble then your sponge is too wet. Simply squeeze out the excess water and re-apply more paint.

3 For a more colourful face add a third border tone and repeat the soft dabbing strokes. The paint dries quickly so you need to be fast when blending to ensure a good coverage. Check that all the edges around the jaw-line are solid and even. If you wish to create a face using different tiers of colour, you will find it is easier to start at the chin.

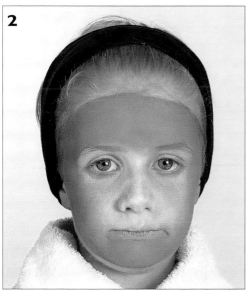

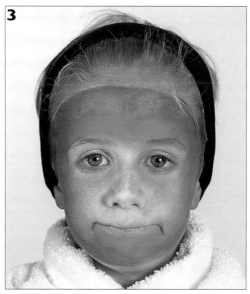

FIELDMOUSE AND BUNNY RABBIT

Animals made popular by cartoons, such as mice and bunnies, are quite easy to face paint. Look closely at animal pictures to find a facial feature that can be exaggerated. To create these faces, the teeth of both the fieldmouse and the rabbit were over-emphasized. Notice how both sets of teeth start from different points – the mouse's teeth are painted from the nose down and the rabbit's from the bottom lip. Adapt the following instructions for the Fieldmouse to create the Bunny Rabbit.

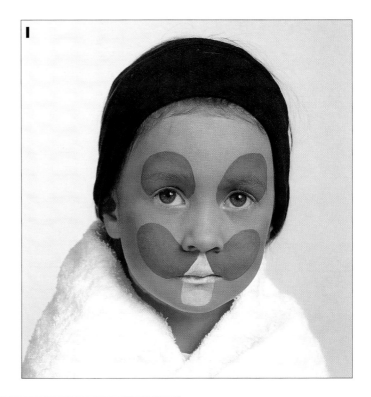

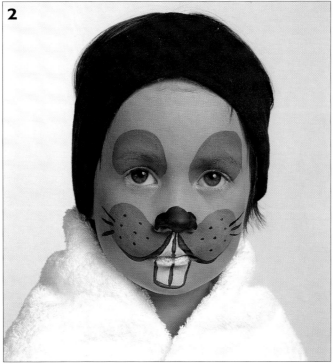

1 Sponge on a skin-coloured base and blush the cheek-bones with pink powder. Using a wide brush, paint a tapered white stripe from the nose down through the mouth and chin. Paint big cir-cles around the eyes in light brown. Add two high curved shapes in the same colour for the cheeks.

2 Outline in black the edge of the lower cheek from under the nose, sweeping up and out along the curve to a point. Still using black, add the whiskers and dots. Carefully outline the large teeth.

AND PLAYFUL PUP

Let your imagination run wild when painting feline faces. Not only can you paint them in their actual browns, oranges and reds, but blues, pinks and greens can be used to good effect to create fun comical cats. The simplest cat or dog only needs a basic black nose and whiskers. For a more elaborate effect add a fluffy muzzle and incorporate some fur-like markings. Notice how tying the young girl's hair into bunches has given the Playful Pup some instant droopy ears.

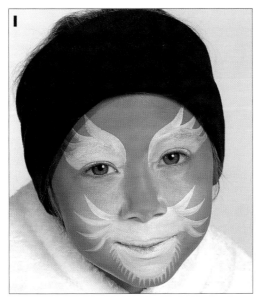

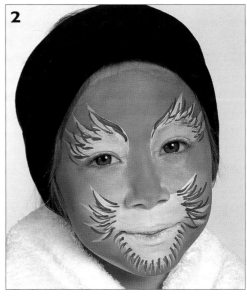

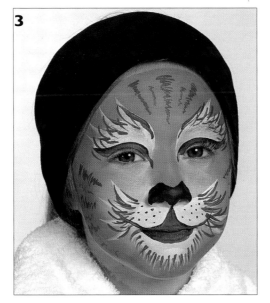

1 Sponge on a full white base and add an orange border tone around the edges and down the nose. Lightly blend in a third tone of red. Paint in the white eye shapes by starting at the inner corners and sweeping the brush up and out to a point. Repeat using similar strokes for the muzzle.

2 Add flecks of red and brown to the outer edges of the white pattern around the eye and muzzle areas to give a fluffy appearance.

3 Now paint some brown wavy fur markings on the forehead and the cheeks. Using black paint, block in the eyelids and the end of the nose. From under the nose, divide the muzzle into two with a wide smile. Colour the bottom lip black and finish with some dots for whiskers.

TIGER

The striking markings of the big cats lend themselves really well to face paints. As tigers, leopards and lions all share basic characteristics you can use the same procedure for the base, eye and muzzle before adding their distinctive fur markings. Paint wavy forked lines onto the face for a tiger, whilst groups of square dots will suggest a leopard's coat. Use long feathery strokes to indicate a lion's shaggy mane.

FABULOUS FAKE FUR
Fake fur is inexpensive and widely available, so why not complete the look with a 'big cat' suit. Make the head in a simple hood-shape, adding two rounded ears.

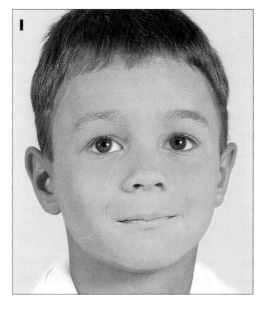

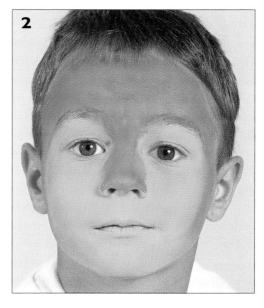

1 Sponge on a yellow base to cover the whole face.

2 Add a border tone of orange to cover the forehead, the nose and the sides of the face.

3 Paint in white zig zag shapes sweeping up from each eye. Create a solid area of white for the muzzle. Sweep two black forked lines up and outwards from each eye. Extend these lines down the sides of the nose. Add black squiggles to the forehead and cheeks to indicate fur markings. To finish, dip a flat-edged brush in black paint, hold it under the nose and flick it upwards to give a furry look. Paint a black line down from the nose and across the upper lip, and add some dots for whiskers.

BIRD OF PARADISE

This beautiful bird of paradise can be painted in a range of different colours. Try using pastel shades of pink, mint and yellow for a soft subtle look. For a striking, dramatic effect, sponge on a three-tiered base in purple, blue and green and then complete with a range of black, gold or silver feathery markings. When using glitter on any face, do take care not to place it too close to the eyes.

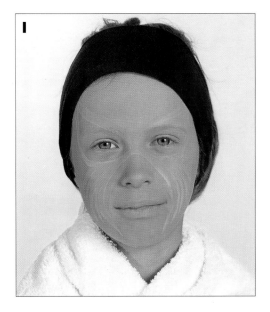

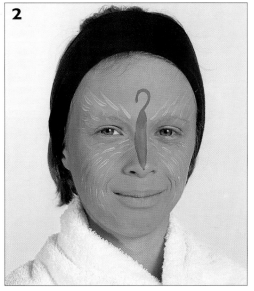

FANCY FEATHERS
Create a fantasy costume to complement your painted face by simply tying a colourful feather boa around your shoulders and adding a feather or two to your hair.

1 Sponge on a skin-coloured base. Using a pale blue, paint the outline of the wings, starting at the nose and sweeping up and out to a point. Then curve this line down under the eyes, before extending long spiky strokes downwards to indicate the outer edges of the lower wings.

2 Using a wide brush, colour the wings in pale blue. Paint a dark blue bird's body down the middle of the nose, adding a hooked head shape in the middle of the forehead. Using yellow paint, dab fine feathery brush strokes at random all over the wings.

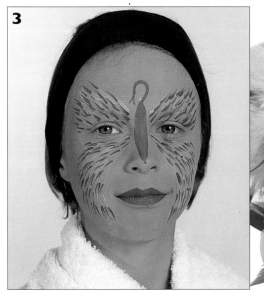

3 Add further feather marks to the wings in red and dark blue. Place a small red beak and white eye dot on the head of the bird. Finally paint the child's mouth red and lavishly dash with glitter.

CREEPY CRAWLY

This creepy face is enough to make anyone's legs start to wobble. By taking a closer look at the creepy crawly world around you, there are all sorts of horrors to draw inspiration from. Try painting that daddy longlegs that climbs up the bath, or maybe just a simple bug on the end of a nose. Don't forget you can always include other small details such as a web or honey pot, to make it that little bit more realistic!

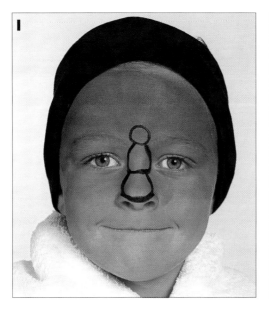

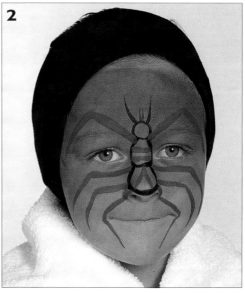

1 Starting at the chin and working upwards, sponge on a three-tiered base in purple, green and yellow. Take care to blend all the edges of the colours together. Paint three circles in black down the nose to form the spider's body.

2 Change to orange and paint some markings across the spider's body. Add the eight legs – one pair above the eyebrows and the other three pairs slanting out from the nose. Add the antennae in black.

3 To make the legs hairy, simply paint small black lines across and down the length of each leg. Finally, colour the body shape in black.

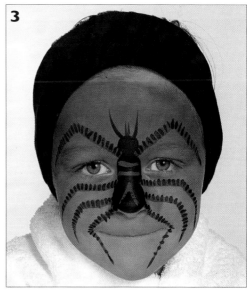

BUTTERFLY

When this brightly painted butterfly shows its face it's obvious that spring cannot be far away! With all sorts of possible colour combinations, matching the colour of the butterfly to the child's clothing can be a pleasing final touch. As an alternative to the design shown here, try painting butterfly motifs on the cheeks or over one eye, perhaps including a garland of flowers.

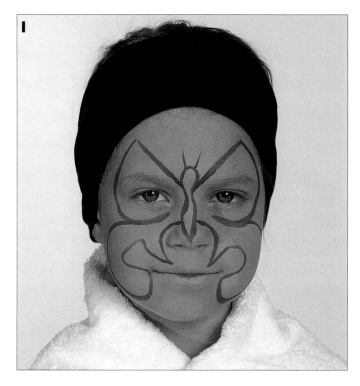

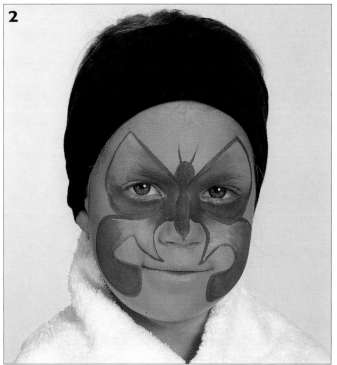

1 Sponge on a skin-coloured base. Using a fine brush outline the butterfly's body, wings and antennae in dark blue. Check that each side of the face is symmetrical.

2 Fill in the butterfly with three complementary colours (purple, bright pink and pale blue were used here). Using a slightly damp brush, blend the colours evenly together.

3 Paint some dark blue scalloped shape markings all over the wings. Scatter some sparkly glitter all over the design. You may also wish to paint the mouth.

SWAN LAKE

The graceful swan, with its elegant simplicity, is another creature that lends itself very well to face painting. Rather than a black swan on a light background, try painting white swans on a dark blue base. Add your own style of floral decoration or perhaps just a few simple swaying grasses. For a romantic touch, paint two facing swans over each eye where they will be seen to be kissing.

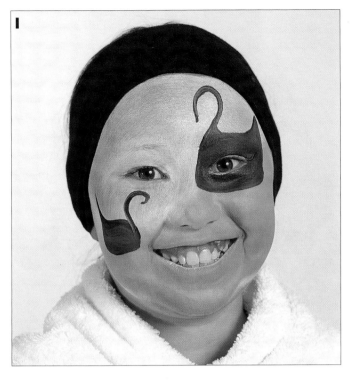

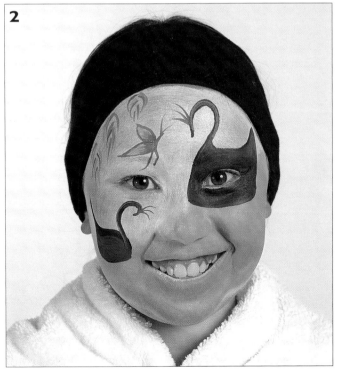

1 Sponge on a full white base. Blend in some green around the chin area. Add pale blue and blend this shade lightly up to one eye. Using a wide brush, paint an oval shape for each swan, bringing the tail end to a point. Add the hooked head and neck.

2 With a fine brush, paint the swan's head crowns in dark blue. Outline a butterfly in dark blue on the forehead, adding multicoloured wings and random sprays of colour as further decorative touches.

3 Adorn the lake with orange and green bull-rushes. Add white feather marks to the swans and ripples to the lake. Paint tiny red beaks on the swans and give the child a prominent red mouth. Sprinkle some glitter sparingly over the final design.

Clowning Around

As clowns come in all shapes and sizes and are known for letting all their emotions show on their faces, there's scope for a great deal of fun in their make-up. Circus clowns can be either happy, sad, angry, pensive, wide-eyed – you name it, the list is endless. If you want to be a sad Pierrot Clown, experiment with a contrasting two-toned base instead of the traditional white make-up. The crazy Circus Clown will look good dressed in any clashing combination of colours. Clowns are ideal for people without much experience of face painting as they are easy to paint on small children and you can achieve the look with just a few basic details.

The instructions shown here are for a simple clown face that will appeal to all ages.

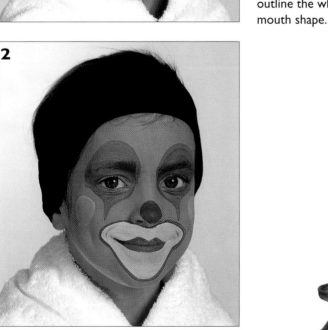

1 This face can be painted with or without a base. Start by painting high arches in green over the eyes. Sweep the colour under the eyes, coming to a centre point. Paint yellow circles on the cheeks.

2 Add a blue border line to the green area around the upper eye. Paint a greatly enlarged white mouth from the tip of the nose, over both the cheeks and chin. Using red, add a small circular nose. Finish by using the red to colour the lips and outline the white mouth shape.

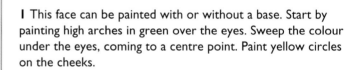

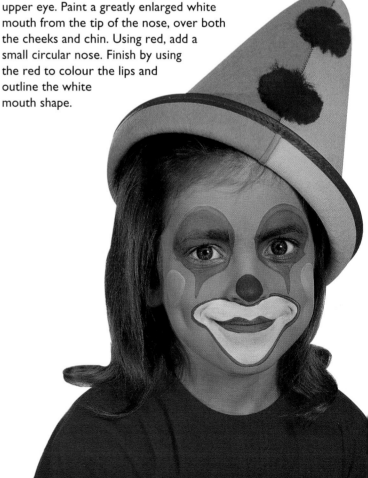

Rag Doll and Army Boy

Toys can provide inspiration for countless different looks. These contrasting faces were based on the favourite toys that young children love to amuse themselves with. However there's nothing to stop you from swapping roles so that the little boy can be made up to look like a favourite rag doll and the girl his army soldier. The camouflage army face is very easy to create and looks particularly effective when buried beneath a matching army cap!

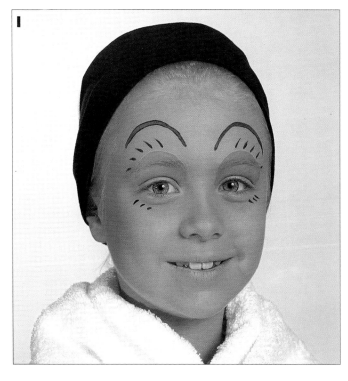

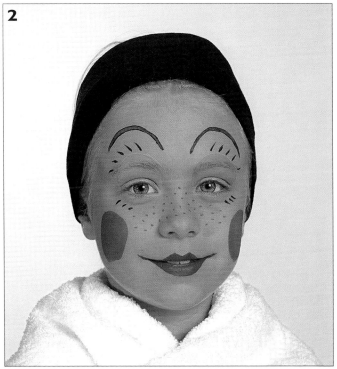

1 Sponge on a skin-coloured base. Paint pale blue arches above the eyes. With a fine brush, paint black wispy eyelashes above and below the eyes. Still using black, paint thin curved eyebrows high up on the forehead.

2 Dab little dots of light brown across the nose to represent freckles. Paint in big round pink cheeks and daub with glitter. Paint the mouth a happy up-turned red. As you can see, the bright yellow wig is the crowning glory of this simple design.

WONDERWEB

Children of all ages love superheroes and nothing will make you more popular than having the power to transform them into their latest hero. Simply by flicking through books, comics, magazines and computer game manuals you will find many faces which can be easily adapted. For a really dramatic touch, extend the colour of the face into the hair by using either a toothbrush or spare sponge loaded with paint.

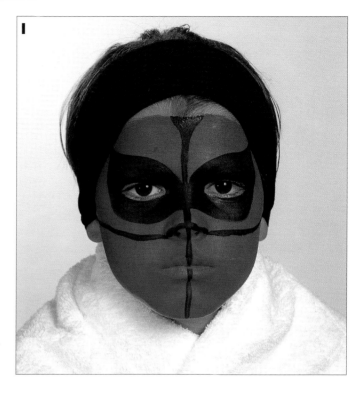

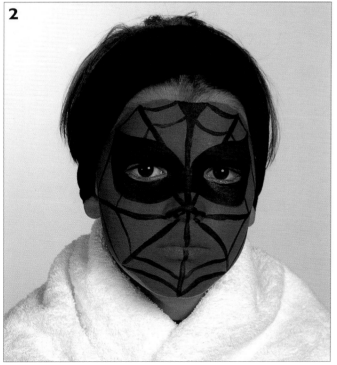

1 Sponge on a dense red base. Around the eyes paint a pointed black mask. With a fine brush, and starting at the forehead, paint a vertical line through the face. Next paint the horizontal line under the mask shape.

2 Continuing with the black paint, separate each quarter of the face again into halves. You will now have eight dividing lines. Lace the web together using a series of curved strokes.

3 Highlight the mask edge in white and place a black spider precariously somewhere within the web.

ICE FAIRY

Legend has it that some fairies can be found at the bottom of the garden under a toadstool – whereas others sparkle and shimmer in a much colder land. To enter the magical kingdom of the Ice Fairy, snow and ice are represented by cool blues, pink and white. For a fire fairy, warm red with yellow and gold to represent flames would work well, while the garden fairy might work best in earthy oranges and browns

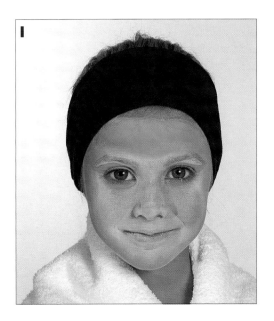

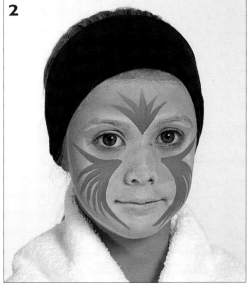

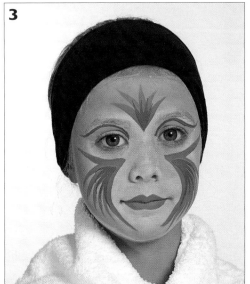

1 Sponge on a pale white base, and blend in a blue border tone. Paint a pale blue wing shape on each eyelid.

2 Dip the brush in bright blue and paint the spiky triangular shapes onto the forehead. Streak a line under the eyes, with a series of similar spiked strokes across the cheeks.

3 Change the colour to bright pink and repeat smaller spiky strokes over the top of the bright blue spikes. Outline the eye shapes in pink. Add a blue mouth and decorate the design with dashes of glitter.

EVIL QUEEN

This simple, yet stunning, Evil Queen works well on both children and adults. The whole appearance hinges on the way the eyebrows are positioned. Look in the mirror and watch how your eyebrows change shape as your expression changes from demure to wicked. Adults could use derma wax or bar soap to smooth down their natural eyebrow hair. Paint a thinner lip line for an even more sinister effect.

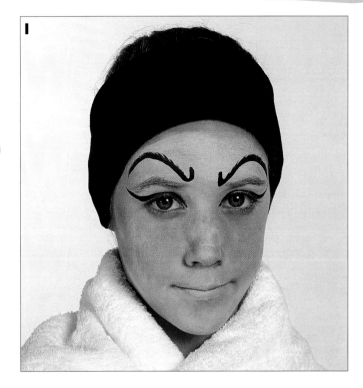

1 Sponge on a pale white base or alternatively a skin-coloured one. Using black, paint in the eyelids, finishing with a dramatic curl. With a fine brush sketch on high arched eyebrow lines and lightly feather the top edges.

2 Paint in the area over the eye sockets in dark blue and add a paler blue up to the shaped eyebrows. Blend the two shades together using a slightly damp brush.

3 Using a blue sparkly powder or dry paint, brush over the cheeks and sides of the nose. Add some dark blue swirling 'tentacles' to the cheeks, ending in a gold glitter dot. Finish with a cold blue mouth.

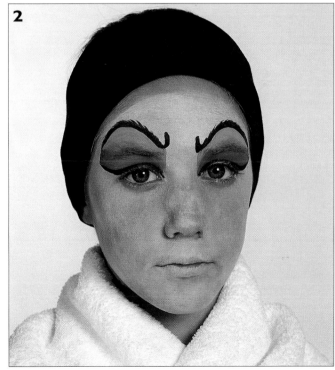

DAYDREAMER

Creating a face based on a fantasy provides endless scope for your imagination as it can take on any shape or form and use any combination of colours, from bright and sharp to soft and hazy. Nothing needs to be symmetrical as to achieve this look, paint marks placed at random work equally well. Coloured hair sprays that wash out will help complete this other-worldly creation.

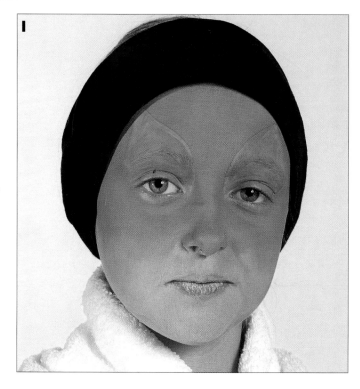

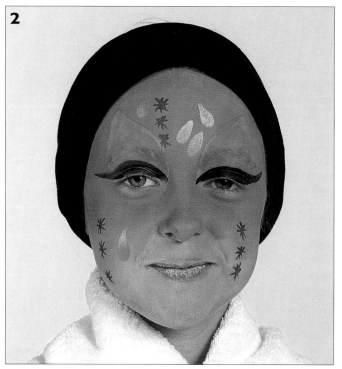

1 Sponge on a two-tiered base in pink and yellow. Alternatively, try using mint and lilac. Paint pale blue high pointed shapes around each eye.

2 Decorate the forehead and cheeks with dark blue stars and gold droplets. Add some sparkling glitter. Paint black wings curling upwards from each eyelid.

3 Using a fine brush, extend the eyeline down the sides of the nose and then streak it back up and outwards. Add some lower lashes. Finally, paint the mouth red.

ELECTRIC SHOCKER

You can achieve startling effects with faces based on different weather. A deep, dark and menacing storm is reflected here in the Electric Shocker. By adding a red line of paint directly under the lower lashes, the eyes appear bloodshot and terrorised. An altogether calmer look can be achieved by painting golden sun rays onto the base, or perhaps a multicoloured rainbow and a pot of gold.

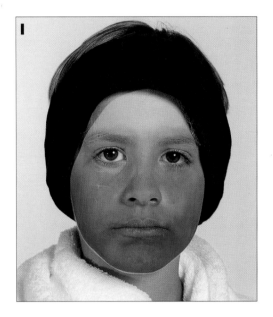

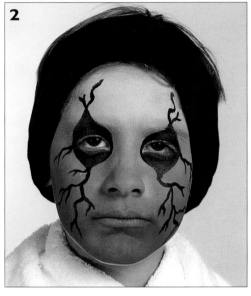

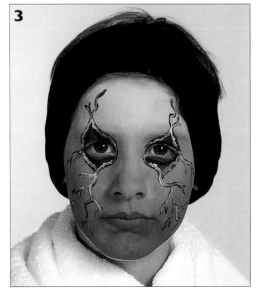

1 Sponge on a three-tiered base in white, pale blue and dark blue. Blend all the edges together.

2 Paint a thin red line under the lower lashes. Change to black and paint the eye patches. Using a fine brush, paint single crooked lines coming out of the eye shapes, adding forked lines at random.

3 Create some lightning flashes by painting white through all the black lines and around the eye patches. Finish with a dramatic black or dark blue mouth.

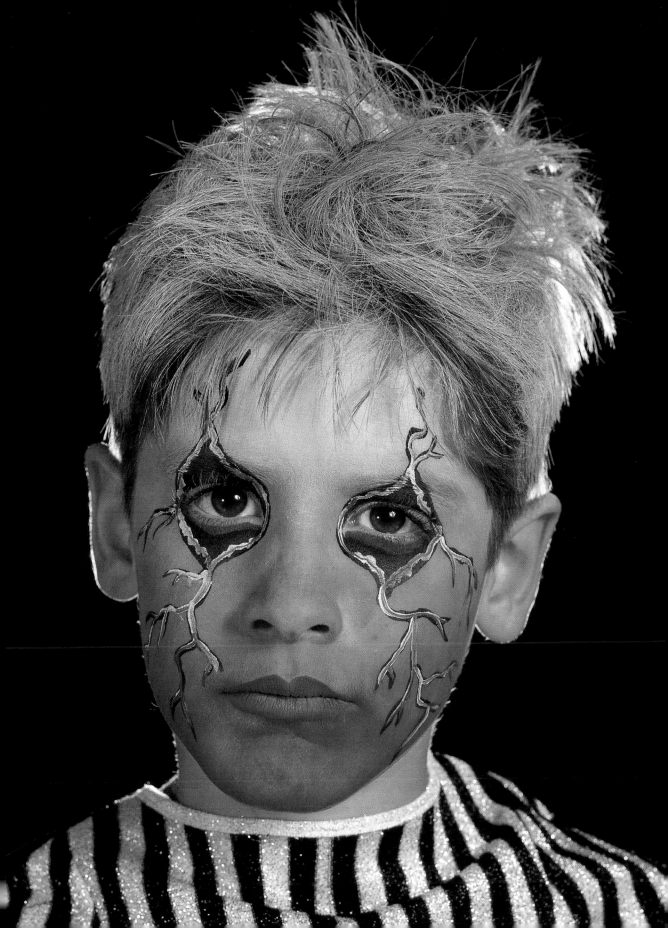

SWEETHEART

Hearts are a symbol of romance and this face would be perfect for Valentine's Day. For a very small child you could paint a simple red heart on each cheek. Note the use of a skin-coloured base which is widely used throughout the book, as it gives a natural complexion to work on, and doesn't distract the eye from the painted design.

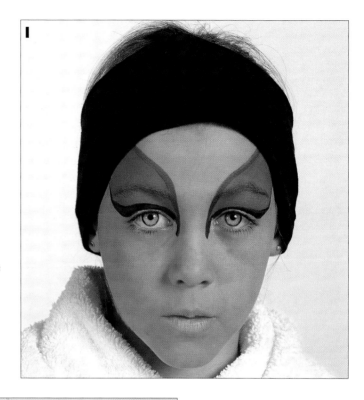

1 Sponge on a skin-coloured base. Paint the black winged shapes above the eye, rising up and out to a point. Echo this shape in bright pink from the eyelids to the either side of the forehead and outline the inner edges in red.

2 Paint hearts on the cheeks and forehead and add a scattering of red glitter. Paint the mouth red and then join the mouth to the cheeks with a sweep of gold glitter.

Sports

If you are interested in sport, there are many different faces that you can paint to show your support. Try painting the particular colours of your favourite hockey, baseball or soccer team on your face to match their kit. You could even add a team name or slogan to your design. Support for a more individual sport, such as tennis, could be shown by a pair of miniature rackets applied to the cheeks. The sports shield on the face of this young football fan would also work well when painted smaller onto the arm as a tattoo.

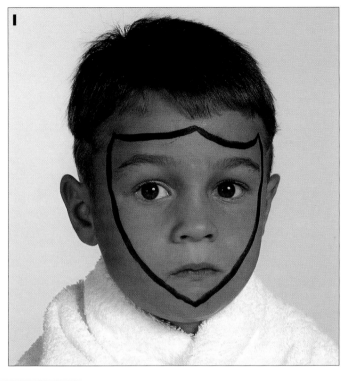

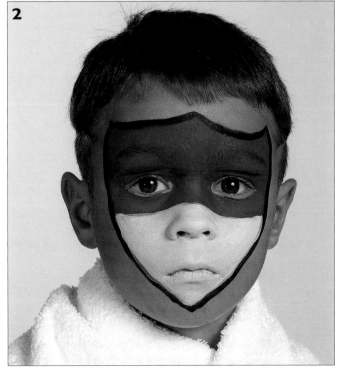

1 Starting at the forehead, outline the shape of the shield in black.

2 Divide the shield into three sections, painting the top part red, the middle blue and the bottom white.

3 Paint wide stripes in red and thinner stripes in blue throughout the white area.

ASTRO AND YIN-YANG

The spiritual side of life can be inspirational for face painting. Depicting the twelve equal constellations of the zodiac, this face draws upon astrology to portray a flaming sun. Using the sun, moon and stars, this Astro face can be re-invented to create endless different looks. Based on the ancient Chinese philosophy of balance, the Yin-Yang face has been painted in pinks and purples, unlike the traditional black and white version.

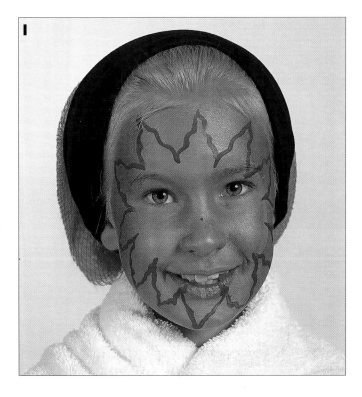

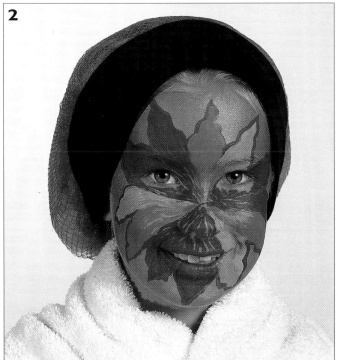

1 Sponge on a gold base. Paint a circle around the face close to the eyes and above the mouth in a skin tone colour. Next divide this circle into twelve equal sections. With dark blue on a fine brush and using your dividing marks, outline the twelve wavy peaks. Place a central blue dot on the nose.

2 Starting at the forehead and rotating clockwise, paint the peaks alternately in blue, yellow, red and purple, lightly sketching each colour towards the central dot. To finish, add a dark blue moon and stars to the design and spangle with glitter.

MASQUERADE

Mimicks Masks are ideal if you would prefer that children did not have lickable painted details around their mouth. Be bold when painting masked faces as I find the darker and more prominent the colours the more stunning the results. You can't go wrong in decorating your mask faces with a sprinkling of glitter or stick-on jewels. You can paint them with or without a base and experiment to create your own designs.

Monster

All small children seem to love being made up to look like four-legged monsters, such as reptiles and dinosaurs. You will be amazed to witness the transformation from an angelic child to a ghastly green, sharp fanged imaginary beast! For by painting distinctive features, like a row of painted teeth onto the face, you quickly lose sight of the child and confront the most frightening and fiendish of faces.

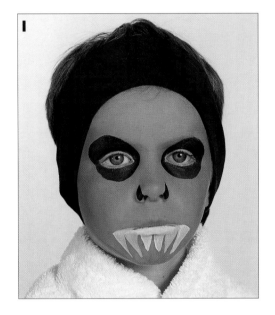

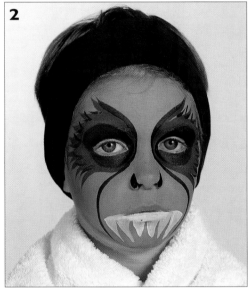

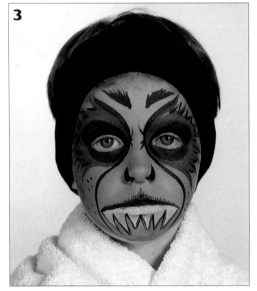

1 Sponge on a green base and stipple yellow down through the middle of the face. Using black, paint solid oval shapes around the eyes and along the edge of the nostrils. Change to white and paint a line along the bottom lip, extending it sideways in each direction. Paint some fangs downwards from this line, coming to a point at the chin.

2 Around the black eyes, paint spiky eye shapes in red. Feather the edges in black and sweep a wavy line down from the eyes to the outer fangs. This will help to bring the centre of the face forward.

3 Still using black, paint a pair of hairy eyebrows and some frown lines between the eyes. Add an extended line of black to the top lip and use thin brush strokes to create the appearance of hair growth. Outline the fangs in black and add some dots to the cheeks.

OGRE

We have all read fairy tales in which ogres were giants who were quite happy to make a meal out of human beings. Unspeakable monsters, they used to go about their business without so much as a thought for their victims. This interpretation presents a very different face of the ogre. Here he is crooked, sullen and confused. Far from just being a cruel monster, his softer side is written all over his face.

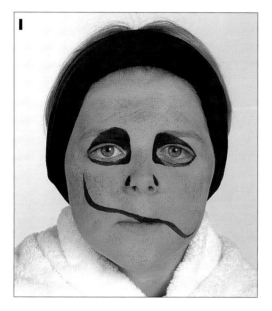

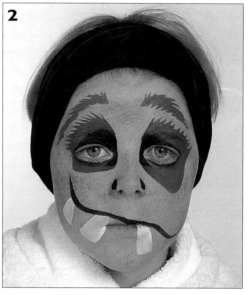

1 Sponge on a yellow base and roughly stipple with some orange blemishes. Give the eyes a soulful look by encircling them in black, squaring up the inner edges against the nose. Add black nostrils and a long lopsided line to represent the mouth.

2 Using a rust colour, paint whiskery eyebrows high on the forehead and a shaggy uneven line around the eye shapes. Paint three broad white teeth to protrude from the black mouth line.

3 Highlight the lower edge of the eye shapes with a white streak. Create a new mouth by filling in the lower lip line in red and outline the bold teeth in black. Finally, add some smudgy black stippling to the face.

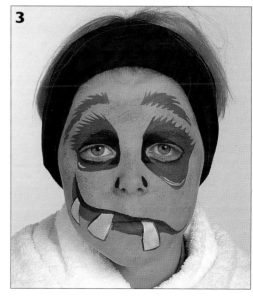

BONES

Ghosts, ghouls and goblins are all things that you hope you won't bump into in the night! Apart from its spooky appeal, children will love this idea for face painting, as with little extra work the whole body can be easily transformed into a skeleton. Perfect for fancy dress parties, simply sketch out the basic bone structure on black paper and fill in the appropriate areas in white paint.

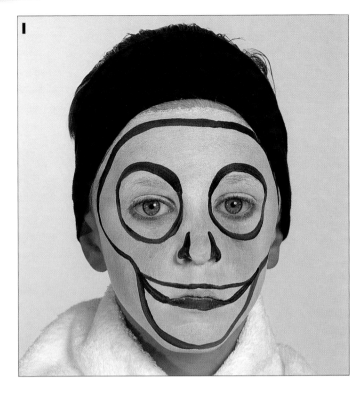

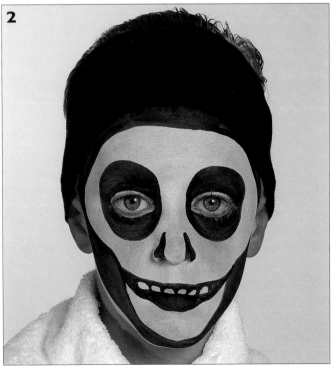

1 Sponge or paint a heavy white base. With black on a brush, outline the eye sockets and nostrils. Paint a skull shape around the edges of the face and draw an elongated mouth across the width of the skull.

2 Using black on a large brush, fill in the solid eye sockets and nostrils. Use black to paint around the outside of the skull shape. If necessary, build up the density with two coats. Add some bony teeth lines.

Nightshade and Werewolf

The eerie world of the supernatural offers up many possibilities for face painting. You will be surprised to discover that the most simple silhouettes and solid black shapes over a multicoloured background can have a spellbinding effect. Equally, the dramatic use of strong black lines to exaggerate the eyebrows and create the fangs on the Werewolf's face are simplicity itself. If you change the base for the Nightshade witch to a plain green one, and add some warts, this face will indeed cast an evil eye.

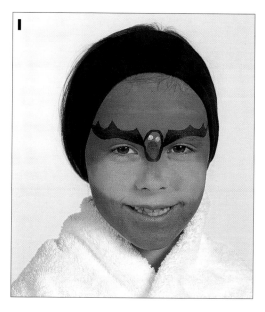

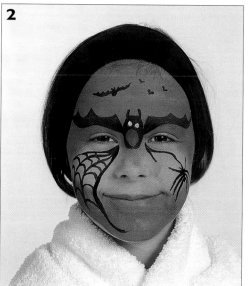

1 Sponge on a four-tiered base in blue, pink, yellow and green. Using black on a brush, outline an oval shape to represent the bat's body on the bridge of the nose. From this sweep a line up and out over the eyebrows, and scallop the top of the wings. Inside the oval, paint a red circle and two smaller white ones.

2 Paint some small black bats across the forehead. Colour in the bat head around the red and white circles and add the ears. From inside one eye, paint four lines downwards and join to form a web. Hang a black spider from the other eye.

3 Add tiny white fangs and small black pupils to the bat's face. Paint the child's mouth black, upturning and downturning alternate corners for a crooked effect. Dab the forehead with silver glitter.

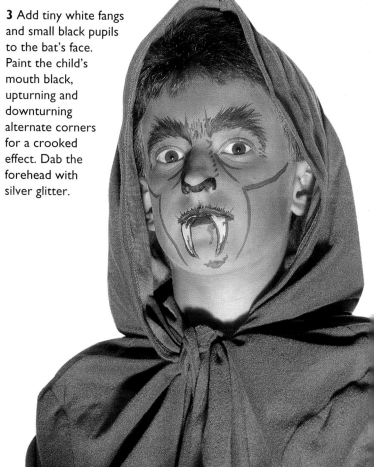

THE LIVING DEAD

To create this nightmare apparition, water colour paint has been made to look like blood, as it is an easy, cheap and safe option for young children. Another possiblity is to buy fake blood capsules, available from most good toy shops and theatrical suppliers. However, if you wish to simulate blood on older children or adults, you could track down 'film blood', a fake blood product used for film and TV work. Try mixing a few coffee granules with it to form lumpy blood clots. Beware of this product as it could irritate the eyes and it can also stain clothing.

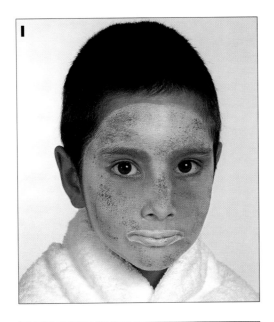

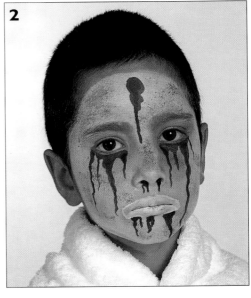

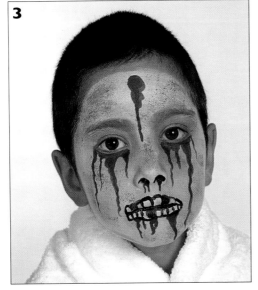

1 Sponge on a patchy white base and lightly stipple some areas with red. Brush on a dark grey powder or dry paint around the eye sockets. Paint a white oblong shape over the mouth and add a touch of yellow to it.

2 With red, paint a bullet hole on the forehead and a line closely under each eye. Paint some lines trickling down from the eyes, nostrils and mouth. You will then need to paint a darker red or brown on top of the flowing blood to give these depth.

3 Using a fine brush with black, outline the mouth and nostrils. Put in the teeth lines and colour over a few to simulate gaps.

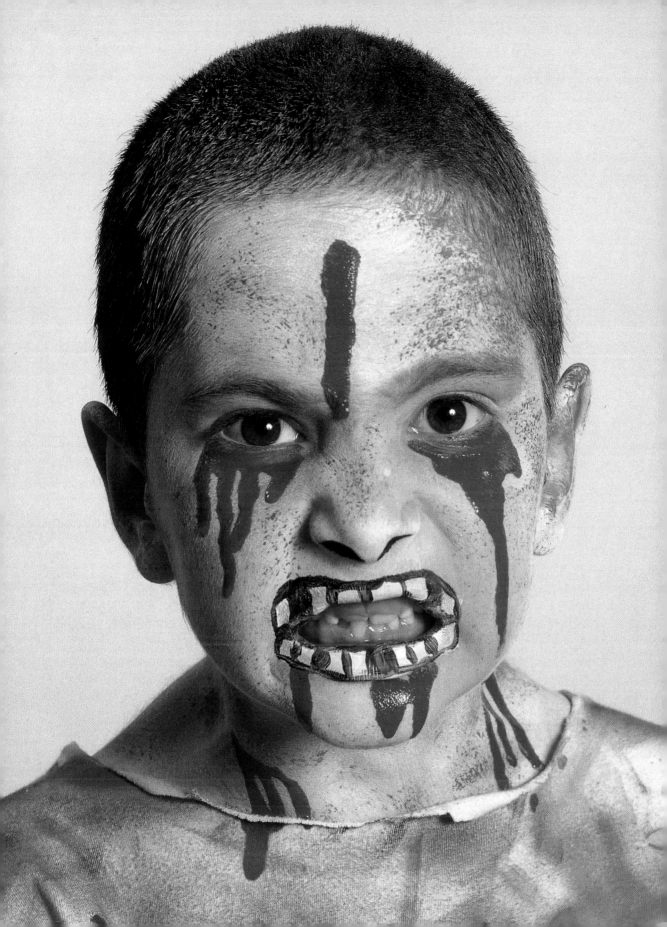

Hands and Feet

By using your imagination, most of the face designs in this book can have co-ordinating hands and feet. The Evil Queen could have her fingers adorned with sparkly rings and colourful bracelets wrapped around her wrists, or you could continue the theme you have painted on your face, as we have shown here with the Tiger's Paw and the Skeleton Hand.

As when painting faces, it is sometimes best to first sponge a base over the area you wish to paint. Allow this to dry before adding your design.

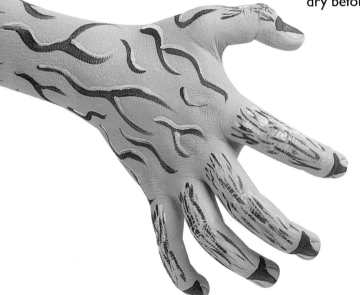

TIGER'S PAW

1 Sponge an orange base over the hands and the lower half of the arms. Allow to dry.

2 Use black and white paints to imitate the tiger's forked, wavy markings, then make short, straight strokes over the fingers to give the impression of fur.

3 Finally, paint sharp black claws over the fingernails. You can adapt this design for other animals.

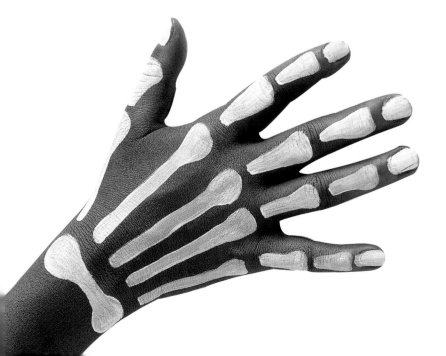

SKELETON HAND

1 Sponge a black base over the hands and the lower half of the arms. Allow to dry.

2 With white paint, make the bone-like shapes over the upper wrists, hands and along each finger.

3 Finish by painting the fingernails white. When you have had some practice you can have a go at painting your whole body!

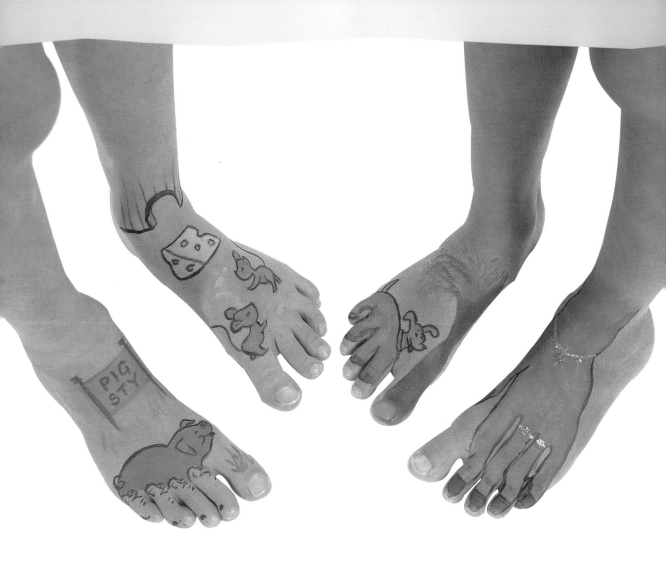

As well as having coordinated hands you can also paint your feet to match the designs on your face. You could give the Ogre green feet with black spiky claws and red veins or paint some clown shoes with colourful bows and stripy socks for the clown. Try painting footwear on feet such as fluffy slippers or baseball boots.

Alternatively, paint a quick amusing scene like the ones above. The joy of this is that you and your friends can have lots of instant fun painting each other's feet with all sorts of designs which you can create yourself.

Tattoos

Do not be put off from trying your hand at these fun tattoos as you do not have to draw directly onto the skin, but have the chance to work out your design on paper first. Big, bold designs with a strong black outline work best as they not only look good but are the easiest to paint. Get inspiration from your children's favourite books, videos and TV programmes.

1 Simply trace your chosen artwork onto tracing paper using a soft pencil. With a wet cotton wool pad, dampen the area of skin and place your transfer on top (pencil side down).

2 Rub the back of the tracing paper with the cotton wool and then peel away to reveal a faint outline for guidance.

3 Using a black make-up pencil, go over the outline of your design – you are then ready to colour in your tattoo.

THE AGEING PROCESS

Making the young look old is a much more fun and rewarding process than watching our own faces age! Cream make-up has been used for this sequence, although water colour paint can be used. Here the years have been added to two children aged 8 and 10 who, dressed in the appropriate clothing, now look like old age pensioners. This make-up is perfect for children playing adult roles in school and drama productions.

Applied quite crudely, this make-up works best at a distance and a more subtle effect would be needed for viewing at a closer proximity. Adapt the colours accordingly for dark skins and use a similar method to age the neck, hands and feet. You can apply skin-coloured water-based paint on a toothbrush to the hair to give a natural greying appearance.

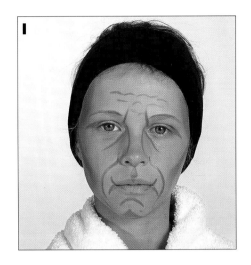

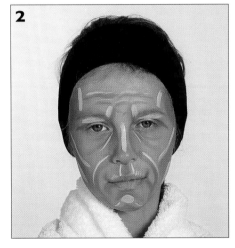

1 Apply a pale foundation thinly over the face with a latex sponge. Change to a medium brown colour and shade the temples, cheekbones and jaw line with your fingertips. Next use a fine brush to add lines to the forehead, eyebrows, eyes, eyebags, sides of the nose, nose hollow, smile lines, corners of the mouth and chin. With a clean dry brush, blend in these shading lines.

2 Now using an ivory colour, add highlights with a brush to the areas you have already shaded. Blend the highlights with another clean dry brush away from the shading. If you are using cream make-up, set each stage of application with a loose translucent powder.

3 Apply a reddish brown colour to the outer eyes, cheeks and chin by brush. Place a very pale line under the lower lashes and a dot on the end of the nose. Stipple the colour with your fingertips. Finally, ask your model to pucker their mouth and sketch lightly through the natural creases in pale brown.

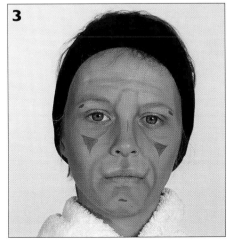

Wounds

If you have ever wondered how they create those gory scenes on television – here's how. With the help of special make-up, you can give rise to a fake wound that will fool your family and friends into rushing for the bandages. Follow the instructions below to create a gruesome knife slash and then use the same techniques to create bullet holes, bruises and other wounds.

The products you will need to create special effects are:

Derma wax

Translucent powder

Cold cream

Film blood (or fake blood capsules from toy and theatrical suppliers)

Water-based paint

Spatula

Stipple sponge

Coffee granules

Orange stick

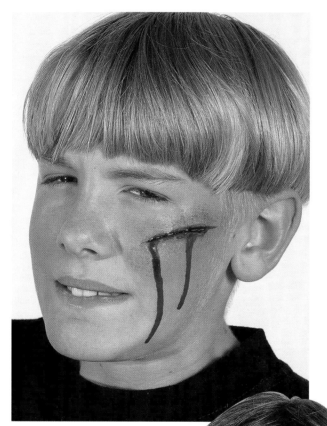

KNIFE SLASH

1 Soften the wax in the tub by scraping the surface with the rounded end of a spatula. Build up a bump on the cheek by pressing small amounts of wax into the skin with the spatula. Blend the wax by dabbing on a little cold cream and use your fingertips to smooth out the edges.

2 With an orange stick, or the end of a brush, cut a crevice into the wax. Take care at this point not to get too close to the underlying skin. Mould and shape the open wound using cold cream and dust lightly with translucent powder.

3 Next use a stipple sponge and lightly apply some red paint to the outside edges to create the effect of bruising. Inside the wound opening, paint the bottom black for depth and red around the edges.

4 Pour some liquid film blood into a lid and add a few coffee granules. Mix together lightly. Pick up these blood clots on a fine brush and position inside the wound. Finally apply some more of this liquid and let it run down the cheeks for a really gory effect!

BULLET WOUND

Using the same techniques as for the knife slash, you can create a realistic bullet hole wound. The effect is made even more dramatic by adding blood clots.

SUPPLIERS AND ACKNOWLEDGMENTS

Thank you to my children who have patiently allowed me to practice on them over the years.

Ashlea Leathem aged 10
Bird of Paradise
Hands and Feet
Ageing girl
Casualty victim

Asa Leathem aged 8
Monster
Circus Clown
Hands and Feet
Ageing boy

and a special big thank you to the children of **St Francis School**, Chandlers Ford, who participated in making this book. They were in alphabetical order:

Jennifer Armstrong aged 5
Mimicks Mask

Laura Armstrong aged 7
Clown

Caroline Barry aged 11
Sweetheart

Rachel Bramham aged 8
Astro

Paul Champion aged 7
Base steps

Samantha Cross aged 10
Daydreamer

Alison Dancey aged 6
Fairy tattoo

Lucy Davis aged 9
Yin-Yang

Alex Dellow aged 5
Bunny Rabbit

Simon Ghafoor aged 6
Living Dead
Parrot Tattoo

Danielle Harder aged 6
Alley Cat

Michael Hatch aged 11
Knife slash victim

Stephen Hatch aged 8
Electric Shocker
Bullet hole victim

Rebecca Hutchinson aged 11
Mimicks Mask

Arron McIntyre aged 7
Tiger
Sports shield

Kirstie McIntyre aged 5
Fieldmouse
Face painters model

William Mason aged 6
Bones

Danny Milczarek aged 10
Casualty victim

Tommy Milczarek aged 8
Casualty victim

Emma Mussell aged 8
Butterfly

Sarah Mussell aged 5
Mimicks Mask

Hayley Parsons aged 10
Evil Queen
Clown tattoo

Nicola Parsons aged 7
Ice Fairy

Victoria Quinn aged 8
Masquerade

Christopher Rees aged 9
Werewolf

James Rimmer aged 5
Creepy Crawly

Natalie Stanton aged 6
Playful Pup

Jade Stewart aged 5
Pierrot clown

Ben Wood aged 8
Wonderweb
Fish tattoo

Luke Wood aged 10
Ogre
Indian tattoo

Katie Yeates aged 9
Mimicks Mask

Fiona Yeoh aged 11
Swan Lake

Victoria Young aged 8
Rag Doll

Tom Young aged 6
Army boy

The costumes were kindly supplied by:

Just for Fun
20 High Street
Eastleigh, Hampshire
(01703) 620664

SUPPLIERS OF FACE PAINTS

United Kingdom

Mimicks, PO Box 116, Eastleigh, Hampshire SO53 4ZN
(01703) 255894

Treasure House of Make-up,
197 Lee Lane, Horwich,
Bolton, BL6 7JD
(01204) 668355

Charles H Fox Ltd,
22 Tavistock Street,
London WC2
(0171) 240 3111

Other Countries

Grimas,
PO Box 3240,
2001 De Haarlem,
The Netherlands

Kryolan Gmbh,
Papierstrasse 10,
D-W1000, Berlin 51,
Germany

Maki
9 Rue Monsart
75009 Paris
France

Matisse Derivan,
1 Northcote Street,
Mortlake, NSW,
Australia

Costume Magic,
1 Howe Street,
Auckland City, Auckland,
New Zealand